The Silent Conversation: Mastering the Art of Body Language

Rami Georgiev

Published by Rami Georgiev, 2023.

While every precaution has been taken in the preparation of this book, the publisher assumes no responsibility for errors or omissions, or for damages resulting from the use of the information contained herein.

THE SILENT CONVERSATION: MASTERING THE ART OF BODY LANGUAGE

First edition. June 25, 2023.

Copyright © 2023 Rami Georgiev.

ISBN: 979-8223387305

Written by Rami Georgiev.

"Your body speaks louder than your words. Learn to master its language, and you hold the key to effective communication." – Rami Georgiev

Dedication:

This book is dedicated to all those who are eager to learn the intricate language of the human body. To the curious minds who understand that communication extends far beyond the spoken word and recognize the power of non-verbal cues in our daily interactions.

To the seekers of knowledge, the enthusiasts of human behavior, and the believers in the transformative potential of effective communication through body language. This book is for you.

May the insights and strategies shared within these pages empower you to navigate the complexities of non-verbal communication with confidence and grace. May you uncover the subtleties of facial expressions, gestures, and postures, and unlock the secrets they hold.

To all those who understand that by mastering the art of body language, we can forge deeper connections, build trust, and convey our true intentions to the world. This book is dedicated to your unwavering curiosity and commitment to personal growth.

Thank you for embarking on this journey with us. Together, let us embrace the silent conversation and discover the profound impact it can have on our lives.

Introduction:

Welcome to "The Silent Conversation: Mastering the Art of Body Language." In a world where communication goes beyond words, understanding the unspoken messages that our bodies convey is paramount. Body language, the silent language of gestures, expressions, and postures, holds the power to shape our interactions, influence perceptions, and build strong connections.

In this eBook, we embark on a journey to unravel the intricacies of body language and equip you with the tools to decode its hidden meanings. Whether you're seeking to improve your personal relationships, excel in professional settings, or simply enhance your overall communication skills, this book offers a comprehensive guide to understanding and utilizing body language to your advantage.

Throughout these pages, we delve into various aspects of body language, exploring the secrets behind facial expressions, gestures, eye contact, and posture. We unravel the fascinating world of microexpressions, examine the significance of body language clusters, and provide practical tips for adapting your own non-verbal cues to communicate with confidence and authenticity.

Furthermore, we address the cultural nuances of body language, recognizing that its meaning can vary across different societies and contexts. We delve into the role of body language in relationships, business settings, public speaking, and even deception detection, empowering you with valuable insights and strategies to navigate these scenarios effectively.

"The Silent Conversation" is not just a passive observation of body language; it is an invitation to actively engage and refine your own non-verbal communication skills. Within these pages, you'll find exercises and practice tips to heighten your awareness of body language, allowing you to cultivate a strong and impactful presence in every interaction.

Remember, the way you present yourself non-verbally speaks volumes about your intentions, emotions, and personality. By mastering the art of body language, you gain a powerful tool to convey your message, build rapport, and create meaningful connections with those around you.

Now, let us embark on this transformative journey through the subtle and expressive world of body language. The silent conversation awaits you.

Chapter 1: The Power of Body Language

Body language, the unspoken language of gestures, expressions, and postures, holds an incredible power in our daily interactions. It is a language that transcends verbal communication, conveying messages that can shape our relationships, influence outcomes, and leave lasting impressions.

In this chapter, we embark on a journey to explore the profound impact of body language and understand why it matters more than we often realize. We will delve into the science behind this silent form of communication, uncovering the ways in which our bodies speak louder than our words.

Within these pages, we will uncover the fascinating research that reveals the significance of body language in various aspects of our lives. From personal relationships to professional settings, body language plays a vital role in how we are perceived and how we connect with others.

We will discover that body language is not limited to specific cultures or regions; it is a universal language understood by people across the globe. We will explore the subtle nuances and variations that exist, recognizing the importance of adapting our body language to different contexts and situations.

Understanding the power of body language allows us to become more effective communicators. By harnessing this knowledge, we gain the ability to align our words with our non-verbal cues, creating a harmonious and compelling message. We can project confidence, build rapport, and establish trust with those around us.

As we embark on this exploration of body language, let us become aware of the impact our non-verbal cues have on our interactions.

Together, we will uncover the hidden meanings behind facial expressions, gestures, and postures, enabling us to unlock the true potential of our communication skills.

Join us on this journey of discovery as we unravel the power of body language and learn to communicate not just with our words, but with the eloquence of our bodies. Prepare to delve into the intricate world of non-verbal communication and uncover the secrets it holds. Let us harness the power of body language and unlock a new level of connection and understanding in our lives.

Why Body Language Matters

IN THIS CHAPTER, WE explore the profound significance of body language and why it matters in our everyday lives. We will delve into the reasons behind its impact on communication, relationships, and overall human interaction. By understanding why body language matters, we can unlock its potential and harness its power to enhance our connections and achieve our goals.

The Non-Verbal Communication Puzzle:

Communication is a complex puzzle, with spoken words representing only a fraction of the message conveyed. Research suggests that a significant portion of our communication—up to 93%—is non-verbal, with body language playing a vital role. While words carry meaning, it is through non-verbal cues that we express emotions, attitudes, and intentions.

The Universality of Body Language:

One compelling reason why body language matters is its universality. Despite cultural differences, humans share common non-verbal cues that transcend language barriers. Facial expressions, hand gestures, and body postures convey emotions, assert dominance or submission, and establish social connections. Understanding these universal signals allows us to navigate various cultural contexts and build rapport with individuals from diverse backgrounds.

Authenticity and Congruence:

Body language provides cues to detect authenticity in communication. When verbal and non-verbal cues align, it enhances trust and credibility. Conversely, incongruence between words and body language raises suspicion and erodes trust. Recognizing and displaying congruent body language enables us to build stronger connections, fostering genuine relationships and effective communication.

Emotional Expression and Empathy:

Emotions are an inherent part of the human experience, and body language is a powerful vehicle for expressing them. Facial expressions, such as a smile or a furrowed brow, convey joy, sadness, anger, or surprise. By being attuned to these cues, we can better understand others' emotional states, show empathy, and respond appropriately, strengthening interpersonal bonds.

Influence and Persuasion:

Mastering body language can enhance our persuasive abilities. Certain non-verbal cues, such as confident posture, eye contact, and assertive gestures, convey authority and influence. By leveraging these signals effectively, we can inspire confidence in others, influence their perceptions, and create a compelling impact in professional and personal settings.

Intuition and Decoding Subtle Cues:

Body language enables us to tap into our intuition and decode subtle cues. Non-verbal signals often convey information that goes beyond what is explicitly said. Microexpressions, fleeting facial expressions lasting a fraction of a second, can reveal concealed emotions or thoughts. By developing our intuition and understanding these subtle cues, we gain insights that enrich our interactions and enable more accurate interpretations.

Relationship Building and Connection:

Body language is an essential tool for building and strengthening relationships. It allows us to establish rapport, foster trust, and deepen connections with others. Active listening, demonstrated through attentive body language, shows respect and interest in the other person, nurturing meaningful relationships both personally and professionally.

Conflict Resolution and Negotiation:

In situations of conflict and negotiation, body language plays a pivotal role. Non-verbal cues can convey assertiveness, openness, or defensiveness, influencing the dynamics of the interaction. Understanding the impact of body language in such contexts empowers us to navigate conflicts effectively, resolve differences, and reach mutually beneficial outcomes.

Conclusion:

Body language matters because it enriches our communication, enables authentic connections, and provides valuable insights into the thoughts and emotions of others. By mastering the language of gestures, postures, and expressions, we gain a powerful tool for effective communication, influence, and building relationships. Understanding why body language matters equips us with the awareness and skills necessary to navigate social interactions with greater finesse and achieve our personal and professional goals.

The Role of Non-Verbal Communication

INTRODUCTION:

In this chapter, we delve into the pivotal role of non-verbal communication in our daily interactions. While verbal communication involves the use of words, non-verbal cues play a significant role in conveying meaning, establishing connections, and expressing emotions. Understanding the multifaceted role of non-verbal communication allows us to become more adept at navigating social dynamics and fostering effective relationships.

The Subtle Language of Non-Verbal Cues:

Non-verbal communication encompasses a wide range of cues, including body language, facial expressions, eye contact, gestures, and tone of voice. These cues complement and often overshadow verbal messages, providing additional layers of meaning and context. By paying attention to these subtleties, we can decode the unspoken language of non-verbal cues and gain deeper insights into the intentions and emotions of others.

Enhancing Understanding and Interpretation:

Non-verbal cues serve as powerful tools for enhancing understanding and interpretation. They provide context, clarify ambiguity, and add emotional depth to verbal messages. For instance, a simple smile accompanying a compliment can convey sincerity and warmth, while crossed arms during a conversation might signal defensiveness or disagreement. By attuning ourselves to these non-verbal cues, we can grasp the true meaning behind the words spoken, leading to more accurate interpretations and reducing misunderstandings.

Emotional Expressions and Empathy:

Non-verbal cues play a vital role in expressing and deciphering emotions. Facial expressions, body posture, and gestures offer glimpses into the emotional state of individuals. Whether it's a beaming smile indicating joy or a furrowed brow signifying concern, these non-verbal cues allow us to connect with others on an emotional level. Additionally, by observing and responding to these cues with empathy, we can establish deeper connections and foster a sense of understanding and support.

Non-Verbal Cues in Social Dynamics:

In social interactions, non-verbal communication heavily influences the dynamics between individuals. It helps establish social hierarchies, signal interest or disinterest, and regulate turn-taking during conversations. For example, maintaining eye contact and using open body postures can convey attentiveness and respect, promoting active engagement and effective communication. Understanding and utilizing these non-verbal cues can enhance our social interactions, making us more adept at navigating various social settings.

Cultural Variations in Non-Verbal Communication:

It is important to note that non-verbal cues are not universally interpreted in the same way across cultures. Different cultures have distinct norms and interpretations of non-verbal cues, which can lead to misunderstandings and misinterpretations. Recognizing and respecting these cultural variations is essential for effective cross-cultural communication. By developing cultural competence, we can navigate diverse cultural contexts with sensitivity, understanding, and adaptability.

Non-Verbal Communication and Influence:

Non-verbal communication plays a significant role in influencing others. It can convey confidence, assertiveness, or charisma, impacting how others perceive and respond to us. By mastering non-verbal cues such as strong body posture, appropriate use of gestures, and maintaining eye contact, we can enhance our persuasive abilities, gain credibility, and inspire trust in both personal and professional settings.

Conclusion:

Non-verbal communication is a rich and multifaceted aspect of human interaction. By recognizing and understanding the role it plays in our daily lives, we can unlock its power to enhance our communication, deepen our connections, and foster meaningful relationships. Paying attention to non-verbal cues allows us to engage in more nuanced and effective communication, leading to greater empathy, understanding, and influence.

Cultural Variations in Body Language

WHILE BODY LANGUAGE is a universal form of communication, its interpretation and significance can vary across different cultures. Understanding these variations is crucial for effective cross-cultural communication, as it allows us to navigate diverse cultural contexts with sensitivity and respect.

Cultural Context and Body Language:

Body language is deeply intertwined with culture, shaped by societal norms, values, and traditions. Different cultures have unique ways of expressing emotions, conveying respect, and establishing social hierarchies through non-verbal cues. For example, direct eye contact may be seen as a sign of confidence and sincerity in some cultures, while it can be considered disrespectful or confrontational in others. By recognizing these cultural nuances, we can adapt our own body language and interpret the cues of others more accurately.

Gestures and Postures:

Gestures and postures are integral components of body language that exhibit cultural variations. The meaning and appropriateness of specific gestures can differ significantly from one culture to another. For instance, a thumbs-up gesture may convey positivity and approval in Western cultures, but in some parts of the Middle East, it can be seen as offensive. Similarly, the posture of bowing is a sign of respect in many East Asian cultures, while it may not hold the same significance in other parts of the world. Understanding these cultural variations helps us avoid misunderstandings and navigate social interactions respectfully.

Facial Expressions:

Facial expressions are universal to some extent, with basic emotions like happiness, sadness, anger, fear, and surprise recognized across cultures. However, cultural norms and display rules influence the intensity, duration, and appropriateness of facial expressions. In some cultures, maintaining a neutral facial expression is valued, while in others, displays of emotion are encouraged. It is essential to consider these cultural variations to interpret facial expressions accurately and respond appropriately in cross-cultural communication.

Proxemics and Personal Space:

The concept of personal space and proxemics—how individuals perceive and use space—varies across cultures. Some cultures emphasize close proximity during conversations, while others prefer more distance. Invading someone's personal space unintentionally can lead to discomfort or offense. Recognizing these cultural variations in proxemics allows us to respect others' boundaries and adapt our own behavior accordingly.

Touch and Contact:

Touch is another aspect of body language that is heavily influenced by culture. Some cultures have a high degree of physical contact during interactions, such as hugs, kisses on the cheek, or handshakes, to express warmth and connection. In contrast, other cultures may have stricter boundaries when it comes to touch. Understanding cultural norms regarding touch helps us navigate physical interactions respectfully, avoiding discomfort or offense.

Overcoming Cultural Barriers:

To overcome cultural barriers in body language, it is crucial to approach cross-cultural communication with curiosity, openness, and a willingness to learn. Developing cultural competence allows us to appreciate and respect the diversity of non-verbal communication styles. By observing, listening, and adapting to the cultural norms of the people we interact with, we can bridge gaps in understanding and foster effective communication across cultures.

Conclusion:

Cultural variations in body language highlight the rich tapestry of human communication. Being aware of these variations enables us to navigate cross-cultural interactions with sensitivity, respect, and open-mindedness. By embracing cultural diversity and understanding the intricacies of non-verbal communication in different cultures, we can foster meaningful connections, build trust, and bridge gaps in understanding. Embracing cultural differences in body language enhances our ability to communicate effectively in a globalized world.

Chapter 2: Decoding Facial Expressions

In this digital age where text messages, emails, and social media interactions dominate our communication landscape, the art of decoding facial expressions remains as crucial as ever. Our faces are powerful tools of non-verbal communication, capable of conveying a vast array of emotions and subtle nuances that words alone cannot capture. Understanding and interpreting facial expressions allow us to gain deeper insights into the thoughts, feelings, and intentions of others, leading to more meaningful connections and effective communication.

Understanding Basic Facial Expressions with Examples

FACIAL EXPRESSIONS are a universal language that transcends cultural boundaries and allows us to communicate our emotions and intentions. In this chapter, we delve into the realm of basic facial expressions, exploring the key emotions they convey and the subtle variations that add depth to our non-verbal communication. By understanding and recognizing these fundamental facial expressions, we gain valuable insights into the inner world of others, fostering empathy, connection, and effective communication.

The Six Basic Facial Expressions:

Research has identified six primary or basic facial expressions that are universally recognized across cultures: happiness, sadness, anger, fear, surprise, and disgust. Each expression has a distinct configuration of facial muscles, resulting in unique visual cues that signify the underlying emotion. Let's explore these expressions in detail, along with real-life examples to illustrate their nuances and contexts.

1. Happiness:

Happiness is characterized by a genuine and joyful expression. It involves a smile, with the corners of the mouth turned upward, and often accompanied by raised cheeks and twinkling eyes. Genuine happiness can be seen when someone receives good news, shares a joyful moment with loved ones, or expresses contentment with their current situation.

Example: A person's face lights up with a broad smile as they reunite with a long-lost friend, radiating genuine happiness and excitement.

2. Sadness:

Sadness is associated with a downcast expression and drooping features. It involves a furrowed brow, lowered corners of the mouth, and possibly teary eyes. Sadness can be observed in response to loss, disappointment, or feelings of loneliness.

Example: A person's face shows a pensive expression with downturned lips and a slight trembling of the chin as they listen to a heart-wrenching story, reflecting empathy and sadness.

3. Anger:

Anger is characterized by intense and focused facial cues. It involves narrowed eyes, a furrowed brow, tense jaw muscles, and a tightened mouth. The overall expression conveys a sense of intensity and assertiveness. Anger can be displayed in response to perceived injustice, frustration, or a threat to one's well-being.

Example: A person's face displays a flushed complexion, tightly clenched fists, and a scowling expression as they confront a situation that goes against their values, demonstrating anger and indignation.

4. Fear:

Fear manifests through widened eyes, raised eyebrows, and an open mouth. The facial expression of fear is often accompanied by a freeze or startle response. The aim is to widen the field of vision to detect potential danger and prepare for self-preservation. Fear can be triggered by actual threats, phobias, or feelings of vulnerability.

Example: A person's face shows widened eyes, raised eyebrows, and a mouth agape as they encounter a sudden loud noise, revealing a startled and fearful response.

5. Surprise:

Surprise is characterized by raised eyebrows, widened eyes, and an open mouth. The expression reflects a moment of astonishment or unexpectedness. Surprise can be positive or negative, depending on the context. It can be elicited by sudden events, unexpected news, or startling experiences.

Example: A person's face exhibits raised eyebrows, widened eyes, and a mouth forming an "O" shape as they open a gift to discover a long-awaited surprise, demonstrating genuine astonishment and delight.

6. Disgust:

Disgust involves a wrinkled nose, curled upper lip, and a slight narrowing of the eyes. It conveys a strong aversion or revulsion towards something unpleasant or offensive. Disgust can be triggered by foul smells, distasteful experiences, or encounters with something morally repugnant.

Example: A person's face shows a crinkled nose and a raised

upper lip as they encounter a pungent odor, expressing disgust and a desire to retreat from the unpleasant sensation.

Understanding Variations and Context:

While the basic facial expressions provide a foundation for understanding emotions, it's important to note that there can be variations and subtle nuances within each expression. Cultural factors, individual differences, and context play a role in shaping the intensity, duration, and accompanying cues of facial expressions. Moreover, people may display blended or mixed emotions, where more than one expression is present simultaneously. Recognizing these variations and considering the context helps us interpret facial expressions accurately and empathetically.

Conclusion:

Understanding basic facial expressions is a key skill for effective communication and building meaningful connections. By familiarizing ourselves with the visual cues associated with happiness, sadness, anger, fear, surprise, and disgust, we gain valuable insights into the emotions and intentions of others. Recognizing and interpreting these expressions allows us to respond with empathy, adjust our own behavior accordingly, and establish stronger interpersonal relationships. As we navigate the complex world of facial expressions, we unlock a deeper understanding of the human experience and foster more authentic and effective communication.

Microexpressions and Their Meanings

IN ADDITION TO THE basic facial expressions, there exists a realm of fleeting and subtle cues known as microexpressions. These microexpressions are momentary flashes of emotions that occur involuntarily and often go unnoticed. In this chapter, we explore the intriguing world of microexpressions, their meanings, and how they provide valuable insights into concealed emotions. By learning to detect and interpret these microexpressions, we sharpen our emotional intelligence and enhance our ability to understand others on a deeper level.

Understanding Microexpressions:

Microexpressions are brief facial expressions that occur within a fraction of a second, revealing true emotions that individuals may consciously or unconsciously attempt to conceal. They are subtle and elusive, requiring keen observation and a trained eye to detect. Microexpressions can occur in response to various stimuli, including unexpected news, moments of tension, or when individuals are trying to suppress their true feelings.

The Seven Universal Microexpressions:

Research has identified seven universal microexpressions that mirror the basic facial expressions: happiness, sadness, anger, fear, surprise, disgust, and contempt. These microexpressions are fleeting glimpses into a person's true emotional state, providing valuable clues about their underlying feelings and thoughts. Let's explore each microexpression in more detail, along with real-life examples to illustrate their significance.

1. Happiness:

A microexpression of happiness can be observed as a momentary upturn of the corners of the mouth, a slight crinkling around the eyes, and a subtle lifting of the cheeks. It often occurs in response to pleasant surprises, positive memories, or genuine moments of joy.

Example: During a serious conversation, a person's face briefly reveals a microexpression of happiness as they recall a heartwarming memory, indicating genuine joy despite the seriousness of the topic.

2. Sadness:

Microexpressions of sadness involve a fleeting downward movement of the corners of the mouth, a subtle drooping of the eyebrows, and a slight tension around the eyes. These microexpressions can reveal suppressed feelings of sadness or moments of emotional vulnerability.

Example: In a group setting, a person's face briefly displays a microexpression of sadness when a sensitive topic is mentioned, indicating an underlying emotional response that they may be trying to hide.

3. Anger:

Microexpressions of anger manifest as a momentary tightening of the lips, a quick narrowing of the eyes, and a subtle tensing of the facial muscles. These microexpressions can indicate suppressed anger, frustration, or a desire to assert dominance.

Example: During a heated discussion, a person's face briefly shows a microexpression of anger, reflecting their true emotional response before they regain control and adopt a more composed expression.

4. Fear:

Microexpressions of fear are characterized by a fleeting widening of the eyes, a quick raising of the eyebrows, and a slight opening of the mouth. These microexpressions signify a momentary sense of alarm, unease, or vulnerability.

Example: While watching a suspenseful movie, a person's face briefly displays a microexpression of fear during a particularly intense scene, indicating their instinctive response to the suspenseful narrative.

5. Surprise:

Microexpressions of surprise involve a momentary widening of the eyes, a rapid raising of the eyebrows, and a subtle opening of the mouth. They indicate brief moments of astonishment, unexpectedness, or anticipation.

Example: As a surprise party is revealed, a person's face briefly exhibits a microexpression of surprise, capturing their genuine reaction before they regain composure and join in the celebration.

6. Disgust:

Microexpressions of disgust appear as a quick wrinkling of the nose, a subtle curling of the upper lip, and a momentary narrowing of the eyes . These microexpressions reveal fleeting moments of revulsion or distaste.

Example: When presented with a disagreeable odor, a person's face briefly displays a microexpression of disgust, indicating their immediate aversion to the unpleasant scent.

7. Contempt:

Microexpressions of contempt are characterized by a brief raising of one corner of the mouth, often accompanied by a slight tightening of the cheek muscles. They signify moments of superiority, disdain, or disregard.

Example: During a discussion, a person's face briefly reveals a microexpression of contempt when they disagree with a particular viewpoint, reflecting their momentary feelings of superiority or dismissal.

Detecting and Interpreting Microexpressions:

Detecting microexpressions requires careful observation and practice. By paying attention to subtle facial cues, rapid changes in expression, and inconsistencies between verbal and non-verbal signals, we can uncover hidden emotions and gain a deeper understanding of others. It is essential to consider the context, individual differences, and potential cultural influences when interpreting microexpressions, as these factors can impact the intensity and duration of the microexpressions.

Conclusion:

Microexpressions offer us glimpses into the true emotions that people often try to conceal. By understanding and interpreting these fleeting facial cues, we enhance our ability to read others accurately, develop empathy, and establish more meaningful connections. Detecting microexpressions requires practice and keen observation, but the insights gained are invaluable. As we become more attuned to the subtle language of microexpressions, we unlock a deeper understanding of human emotions and cultivate stronger interpersonal relationships.

Reading Emotions through Facial Cues

INTRODUCTION:

Our faces are intricate canvases that paint a vivid picture of our emotions. In this chapter, we explore the art of reading emotions through facial cues, examining the various components that contribute to our ability to interpret and understand the feelings of others. By honing our skills in reading facial expressions, we unlock a deeper level of empathy, forge stronger connections, and navigate the complexities of human emotions with greater insight.

The Language of Facial Cues:

Facial cues are the subtle shifts and expressions that play across our faces, conveying a wealth of emotional information. These cues include facial expressions, eye movements, eyebrow positions, microexpressions, and other non-verbal signals that work together to create a comprehensive emotional language. By learning to decipher these cues, we gain access to a treasure trove of insight into the emotional states of those around us.

Recognizing Basic Facial Expressions:

The foundation of reading emotions through facial cues lies in recognizing and interpreting the basic facial expressions: happiness, sadness, anger, fear, surprise, disgust, and contempt. Each expression carries distinct visual cues that allow us to identify the corresponding emotion. By observing the positioning of the eyebrows, the movement of the mouth and eyes, and the overall muscle tension in the face, we can decipher the underlying emotions being displayed.

Example: A person's face displays raised eyebrows, widened eyes, and a broad smile, indicating the basic facial expression of happiness. This could suggest that they are experiencing genuine joy or contentment.

Decoding Microexpressions:

Microexpressions are fleeting and involuntary facial expressions that occur within a fraction of a second. They provide glimpses into the true emotions individuals may be attempting to hide or suppress. Recognizing microexpressions requires acute observation and an understanding of the subtle muscle movements that occur in the face. By studying the nuances of microexpressions, we can uncover concealed emotions and gain a deeper understanding of the emotional landscape.

Example: During a conversation, a person's face momentarily exhibits a flash of anger—a microexpression characterized by tightened lips, narrowed eyes, and a tense facial expression. This fleeting expression reveals their true emotional response before they regain composure.

Interpreting Facial Cues in Context:

Reading emotions through facial cues goes beyond recognizing individual expressions. It involves considering the context in which these cues occur, as well as the accompanying verbal and non-verbal signals. Context can significantly influence the interpretation of facial cues, as different situations elicit varying emotional responses. Additionally, cultural and individual differences must be taken into account when interpreting facial cues, as these factors can shape the way emotions are expressed and perceived.

Example: A person's face shows a furrowed brow and downturned lips, which are typically associated with sadness. However, by considering the context—a funeral—it becomes apparent that the expression aligns with the expected emotional response to the somber event.

Combining Facial Cues with Body Language:

Facial cues do not exist in isolation but are part of a larger tapestry of non-verbal communication that includes body language, gestures, and vocal tone. To gain a comprehensive understanding of someone's emotions, it is essential to observe and interpret these cues holistically. By paying attention to the alignment or discordance between facial cues and other non-verbal signals, we can uncover subtle nuances and gain a more accurate perception of the emotional state.

Example: A person's face displays a smile, but their crossed arms and tense posture indicate a sense of defensiveness or discomfort. By combining the facial cue with the body language, it becomes evident that their true emotional state may differ from the surface expression.

Developing Empathy and Connection:

Reading emotions through facial cues is not merely an exercise in observation; it is a gateway to empathy and connection.

When we can accurately interpret the emotions of others, we develop a deeper understanding of their experiences, needs, and desires. This understanding fosters empathy, enabling us to respond with sensitivity and compassion. By actively engaging in the reading of facial cues, we cultivate meaningful connections and create a more harmonious social environment.

Conclusion:

The ability to read emotions through facial cues is a powerful skill that enhances our interpersonal relationships and deepens our understanding of others. By recognizing and interpreting basic facial expressions, microexpressions, and the complex interplay of facial cues, we gain valuable insights into the emotional states of those around us. Reading emotions through facial cues requires keen observation, contextual understanding, and the ability to integrate facial cues with other non-verbal signals. As we hone our skills in reading facial cues, we unlock a deeper level of empathy, forging connections that transcend words and enriching our interactions with others.

Chapter 3: Mastering Gestures and Posture

I n this chapter, we delve into the fascinating realm of body language, exploring the intricate ways in which our gestures and posture convey meaning, influence interactions, and shape our overall communication style. By understanding and harnessing the power of body language, we can elevate our communication skills, project confidence, and establish strong connections with others.

Common Hand Gestures and Their Interpretations

OUR HANDS ARE INCREDIBLY expressive tools that can convey a multitude of messages through gestures. In this chapter, we explore the world of hand gestures—their meanings, interpretations, and the cultural nuances that shape their significance. By understanding the common hand gestures used in communication, we can decode hidden messages, bridge language barriers, and enhance our ability to connect with others on a deeper level.

The Power of Hand Gestures:

Hand gestures are a universal language that transcends words. They add depth, emphasis, and clarity to our verbal messages, amplifying our communication and making it more engaging. From a simple thumbs-up to intricate movements, our hands serve as powerful tools for expression, conveying emotions, intentions, and emphasis. By harnessing the power of hand gestures, we can enhance our communication skills and create a lasting impact on those around us.

Interpretation of Common Hand Gestures:

1. Thumbs-up: The thumbs-up gesture signifies approval, agreement, or reassurance. It is a positive gesture that conveys encouragement and support.

2. Pointing: Pointing with the index finger directs attention or indicates a specific object or person. It can convey emphasis, clarification, or a request for focus.

3. Handshake: A firm handshake is a common gesture used during introductions and signifies trust, respect, and goodwill. It establishes a connection and sets the tone for further interaction.

4. Open Palms: Open palms facing upward are a gesture of openness, honesty, and vulnerability. They signal receptiveness and a willingness to listen or receive.

5. Closed Fist: A closed fist can convey determination, solidarity, or anger, depending on the context. It can be used to express resolve or to symbolize unity.

6. Waving: Waving involves a back-and-forth motion of the hand and is typically used as a greeting or farewell gesture. It denotes friendliness, acknowledgement, or a desire to attract attention.

7. Nodding: Nodding the head up and down signifies agreement, understanding, or affirmation. It is a non-verbal way of saying "yes" and indicates receptiveness to the speaker's message.

8. Crossing Arms: Crossing the arms over the chest can indicate defensiveness, disagreement, or a desire to create physical and emotional barriers. It can also be a self-soothing gesture.

9. Finger Tapping: Tapping the fingers on a surface indicates impatience, restlessness, or frustration. It conveys a desire for action or a need for the situation to progress.

10. Hand-to-Cheek Gesture: Placing the hand on the cheek or chin suggests thoughtfulness, contemplation, or a moment of reflection. It is often seen when individuals are deep in thought or considering a decision.

Cultural Variations in Hand Gestures:

It is important to note that the interpretation of hand gestures can vary across cultures. What may be considered acceptable or meaningful in one culture may have different connotations in another. Cultural norms, beliefs, and customs heavily influence the significance and appropriateness of specific hand gestures. Therefore, it is crucial to approach cross-cultural communication with sensitivity, awareness, and a willingness to adapt our gestures accordingly.

Developing Awareness and Sensitivity:

To effectively utilize and interpret hand gestures, it is essential to develop awareness and sensitivity to the non-verbal cues of others. Paying attention to the context, accompanying body language, and the overall communication dynamic helps us decode the intended meaning behind the gestures. By observing and adapting to the gestures of others, we foster understanding and establish stronger connections.

Practicing Effective Hand Gestures:

To master the art of hand gestures, practice and refinement are key. Observe influential communicators, public

speakers, or actors who effectively utilize hand gestures to enhance their messages. Experiment with different gestures to find ones that feel natural and align with your intended meaning. Seek feedback from others to ensure that your gestures are clear, appropriate, and in harmony with your verbal communication.

Conclusion:

Hand gestures are a powerful form of non-verbal communication that can enrich our interactions and bridge gaps in understanding. By understanding the interpretations of common hand gestures, recognizing cultural variations, and developing sensitivity to the non-verbal cues of others, we enhance our ability to communicate effectively and create meaningful connections. Embrace the expressive potential of your hands, and let your gestures speak volumes in your interpersonal interactions.

Body Posture and Its Implications

OUR BODY POSTURE SPEAKS volumes about our state of mind, confidence, and intentions. In this chapter, we delve into the fascinating world of body posture and explore how it influences our interactions, shapes perceptions, and conveys hidden messages. By understanding the implications of body posture, we can consciously use it to project confidence, establish rapport, and enhance our overall communication effectiveness.

The Language of Body Posture:

Body posture refers to the position and alignment of our body, including the orientation of our head, shoulders, back, and limbs. It is a non-verbal language that communicates our attitudes, emotions, and levels of engagement. Whether we slouch or stand tall, cross our arms or open them, our body posture silently communicates a wealth of information to others. By becoming aware of our own body posture and deciphering the postures of others, we can gain valuable insights into their thoughts and feelings.

Implications of Body Posture:

1. Confidence and Power: A strong, upright posture with an open chest and squared shoulders exudes confidence and assertiveness. It communicates self-assuredness and a sense of authority. Conversely, slouching or hunching indicates a lack of confidence and can diminish our perceived power.

2. Approachability and Openness: Keeping our body relaxed and open, with uncrossed arms and an inviting stance, signals approachability. It conveys a willingness to engage in conversation, listen actively, and establish connections. Conversely, closed-off postures, such as crossed arms or crossed legs, create a barrier and can make others perceive us as unapproachable.

3. Engagement and Interest: Leaning slightly forward, maintaining eye contact, and nodding in agreement demonstrate active engagement and interest in the conversation. These postures show that we are

attentive and invested in the interaction. On the other hand, leaning back, avoiding eye contact, or fidgeting can convey disinterest or boredom.

4. Emotional States: Body posture can reflect our emotional states. For example, slumping shoulders and a drooping head may indicate sadness or defeat. On the contrary, an upright posture with a lifted chin and a spring in our step may signify happiness or enthusiasm. By observing the body postures of others, we can gain insights into their emotional well-being.

5. Authority and Leadership: Adopting expansive postures, such as standing tall with arms outstretched or placing hands on hips, signals authority and leadership. These power poses convey confidence, assertiveness, and a sense of command. They can influence how others perceive us and establish our presence in a group or professional setting.

6. Nervousness and Insecurity: Body postures can also betray nervousness or insecurity. For instance, fidgeting, avoiding eye contact, or excessively shifting weight from one foot to another may indicate discomfort or unease. Being aware of these subtle signs allows us to manage our own body language and project a more confident image.

7. Cultural Variations: It's important to recognize that body posture can be influenced by cultural norms and upbringing. Different cultures have unique expectations and interpretations of body language. For instance, the appropriate distance for personal space and the level of physical contact can vary significantly. When interacting with individuals from diverse cultural backgrounds, it's crucial to be mindful of these variations to avoid misunderstandings.

Harnessing the Power of Body Posture:

By consciously adjusting our body posture, we can positively impact our communication effectiveness. Practicing good posture, such as standing or sitting upright, can enhance our self-confidence, influence how others perceive us, and create a positive impression. Additionally, mirroring the body posture of others in a respectful and subtle manner can foster rapport and create a sense of connection.

Conclusion:

Body posture is a powerful non-verbal communication tool that shapes our interactions, conveys messages, and influences perceptions. By understanding the implications of body posture, we can leverage this language to project confidence, openness, and engagement. Developing self-awareness of our own body posture and attuning ourselves to the postures of others allow us to establish stronger connections, foster empathy, and navigate social situations with greater effectiveness. Let your body posture become an ally in your communication journey, amplifying your messages and creating lasting impressions.

Open vs. Closed Body Language

OUR BODY LANGUAGE HAS the power to speak volumes about our thoughts, emotions, and intentions. In this chapter, we explore the concept of open versus closed body language and delve into its significance in communication. By understanding the subtle cues and signals associated with open and closed body language, we can enhance our interpersonal interactions, build trust, and create a more positive and inclusive environment.

Understanding Open Body Language:

Open body language is characterized by gestures and postures that convey a sense of receptiveness, approachability, and transparency. When we exhibit open body language, we create a welcoming and inviting atmosphere for others to engage with us. Here are some key elements of open body language:

1. Uncrossed Arms and Legs: Keeping our arms relaxed and our legs uncrossed signals openness and a willingness to receive information or connect with others. It demonstrates that we are open to different perspectives and receptive to new ideas.

2. Open Palm Gestures: Using open palm gestures, such as extending a hand for a handshake or gesturing with palms facing upward, conveys trust and honesty. It suggests that we have nothing to hide and are willing to be vulnerable in our interactions.

3. Leaning Forward: Leaning slightly forward while engaged in conversation demonstrates interest and active listening. It shows that we are fully present and invested in what the other person is saying, fostering a deeper connection.

4. Maintaining Eye Contact: Sustaining appropriate and comfortable eye contact indicates attentiveness and sincerity. It demonstrates that we value the person and the conversation, promoting trust and understanding.

5. Relaxed Posture: A relaxed and open posture, with shoulders back and head held high, communicates confidence and approachability. It

creates a positive impression and encourages others to feel comfortable and open in their own communication.

Implications of Open Body Language:

Open body language has several positive implications for communication and relationship-building:

1. Trust and Rapport: Open body language helps establish trust and build rapport with others. It creates an environment of safety and authenticity, allowing for more open and meaningful interactions.

2. Collaboration and Cooperation: When we exhibit open body language, we encourage collaboration and cooperation. It fosters a sense of teamwork and inclusivity, making others feel valued and appreciated.

3. Effective Communication: Open body language enhances the effectiveness of communication. It promotes active listening, empathy, and understanding, enabling us to convey our messages more clearly and receive information more accurately.

Understanding Closed Body Language:

Closed body language, on the other hand, conveys a sense of defensiveness, detachment, or reservation. It creates a barrier between individuals and inhibits the flow of communication. Recognizing the following elements of closed body language can help us understand its implications:

1. Crossed Arms and Legs: Crossing our arms or legs can create a physical barrier and signify defensiveness or a desire to protect ourselves. It can also indicate disagreement or disinterest in the conversation.

2. Tightly Clenched Hands: Clenching our hands tightly or forming fists can communicate tension, frustration, or anger. It suggests that we are on the defensive and not open to dialogue or collaboration.

3. Avoiding Eye Contact: Avoiding eye contact or constantly shifting gaze can indicate discomfort, lack of trust, or a desire to disengage from the conversation. It hinders the establishment of connection and understanding.

4. Leaning Back or Away: Leaning back or away from the person we are communicating with suggests a desire to create distance and emotional detachment. It can signal disinterest or a lack of engagement.

5. Tense or Hunched Posture: Having a tense or hunched posture conveys unease, insecurity, or a desire to protect oneself. It can create a negative impression and inhibit effective communication

.

Overcoming Closed Body Language:

It is important to recognize when we exhibit closed body language and make efforts to overcome it. By consciously adopting open body language, we can improve our communication skills and create a more positive environment:

1. Self-Awareness: Developing self-awareness allows us to recognize our own patterns of closed body language. Pay attention to your posture, gestures, and facial expressions to identify any signs of defensiveness or detachment.

2. Relaxation Techniques: Practice relaxation techniques, such as deep breathing or mindfulness exercises, to reduce tension and promote a more open and receptive state of mind and body.

3. Active Listening: Engage in active listening by maintaining eye contact, nodding, and providing verbal and non-verbal cues that show your interest and attentiveness.

4. Empathy and Understanding: Cultivate empathy and understanding towards others. Put yourself in their shoes and strive to create an environment where everyone feels heard, respected, and valued.

5. Practice and Feedback: Regularly practice open body language in various social situations. Seek feedback from trusted individuals who can provide insights and suggestions for improvement.

Conclusion:

Open and closed body language play a significant role in our communication and interpersonal relationships. By understanding the implications of these non-verbal cues and consciously adopting open body language, we can foster trust, build stronger connections, and create a more inclusive and positive communication environment. Let your body language reflect your openness, receptiveness, and genuine interest in others, and watch as your relationships and interactions flourish.

Chapter 4: Speaking with Your Eyes

They say that eyes are the windows to the soul, and indeed, our eyes have a remarkable ability to convey thoughts, emotions, and intentions without uttering a single word. In this chapter, we explore the captivating art of speaking with your eyes—a form of non-verbal communication that can deeply impact our interactions and forge meaningful connections. By understanding the power of eye contact, eye movements, and expressions, we can master the art of using our eyes to communicate effectively and authentically.

The Power of Eye Communication:

Our eyes have a unique ability to convey a multitude of messages, transcending language barriers and cultural differences. Through eye contact, we establish connections, convey emotions, and express our attentiveness to others. Whether it's a warm gaze that conveys empathy, a confident look that commands attention, or a subtle glance that communicates interest, our eyes hold immense power in the realm of communication.

The Significance of Eye Contact:

Eye contact forms the foundation of effective eye communication. It is a universal signal that shows our presence, engagement, and respect for the person we are communicating with. Maintaining appropriate and comfortable eye contact fosters trust, enhances understanding, and validates the importance of the conversation. It is a non-verbal cue that assures others of our attentiveness and willingness to connect.

The Language of Eye Contact

THE EYES, OFTEN REFERRED to as the windows to the soul, have a remarkable ability to convey a myriad of messages without uttering a single word. In this chapter, we delve into the fascinating realm of eye contact—the silent language that can deeply influence our interactions and relationships. By understanding the nuances of eye contact and its varied meanings, we can harness its power to communicate effectively, build connections, and foster understanding.

The Power of Eye Contact:

Eye contact forms the foundation of non-verbal communication. It is a universal and instinctive way of connecting with others, conveying interest, establishing rapport, and validating the importance of the conversation. The power of eye contact lies in its ability to evoke emotions, create trust, and facilitate meaningful exchanges. Let's explore the language of eye contact in more detail.

1. Intimate Eye Contact:

Intimate eye contact is characterized by close proximity and sustained gaze. It is typically reserved for close relationships or intimate settings. This level of eye contact can convey a deep emotional connection, affection, and desire. For example, when a couple gazes into each other's eyes, it expresses love, passion, and intimacy.

2. Social Eye Contact:

Social eye contact is appropriate for casual interactions and conversations with acquaintances, colleagues, or strangers. It involves making brief, intermittent eye contact to acknowledge the presence of the other person and demonstrate engagement. Maintaining social eye contact shows respect, attentiveness, and openness to the conversation.

3. Assertive Eye Contact:

Assertive eye contact is characterized by a direct, unwavering gaze. It is often used to establish dominance, assert authority, or command attention. For example, in professional settings, maintaining assertive eye contact during negotiations or presentations conveys confidence, credibility, and control.

4. Averting Eye Contact:

Averting eye contact, whether intentional or unintentional, can have various implications. It can signify shyness, submissiveness, or discomfort in certain situations. Conversely, it can also convey disinterest, deception, or a desire to avoid engagement. Understanding the context and accompanying body language is essential to interpret the true meaning behind the aversion of eye contact.

5. Gazing Patterns:

The direction and focus of our gaze can also convey specific messages. For instance:

a. Visual Scanning: When we engage in visual scanning, our gaze moves across different objects or people. This indicates curiosity, observation, or an active search for information.

b. Glances: Brief glances can communicate interest, curiosity, or attraction. They are often used to discreetly assess someone or something without appearing too forward.

c. Prolonged Staring: Prolonged staring can be uncomfortable or intimidating, but it can also convey intense focus, intrigue, or admiration. The context and relationship dynamics are important factors in interpreting the meaning behind prolonged staring.

6. Cultural Variations:

It is important to note that eye contact norms and interpretations can vary across cultures. In some cultures, prolonged eye contact is valued as a sign of respect, while in others, it may be considered impolite or confrontational. It is crucial to be sensitive to these cultural variations when engaging in cross-cultural interactions.

Examples of Eye Contact:

Let's explore some examples that illustrate the language of eye contact:

1. Job Interview: During a job interview, maintaining strong, direct eye contact with the interviewer demonstrates confidence, attentiveness, and sincerity. It conveys your interest in the position and your ability to engage effectively.

2. Public Speaking: When delivering a speech or presentation, making eye contact with the audience members helps establish a connection and keeps them engaged. It conveys authenticity, credibility, and a genuine desire to connect with the listeners.

3. Romantic Interest:

In a romantic context, prolonged eye contact combined with a gentle smile can communicate attraction and interest. It creates a sense of intimacy and emotional connection between two individuals.

4. Negotiations: In a negotiation scenario, maintaining assertive eye contact can convey confidence and assertiveness. It shows that you are determined and resolute in your position, which can influence the dynamics of the negotiation process.

5. Active Listening: When engaged in a conversation, maintaining consistent eye contact with the speaker signals active listening and genuine interest. It demonstrates respect, empathy, and an openness to understanding the speaker's perspective.

Conclusion:

The language of eye contact is a powerful tool in our interpersonal communication repertoire. By understanding its nuances, we can convey emotions, establish connections, and enhance the effectiveness of our interactions. Whether it's through intimate eye contact, assertive gazes, or social acknowledgments, our eyes have the capacity to express a wealth of messages that go beyond words. Embrace the power of eye contact and let your eyes speak volumes, fostering deeper connections and enriching your communication experiences.

Eye Movement Patterns and their Significance

OUR EYES ARE NOT ONLY powerful in their ability to convey messages through eye contact, but they also possess the capacity to communicate through various eye movement patterns. In this chapter, we delve into the fascinating world of eye movements and explore their significance in non-verbal communication. By understanding the different eye movement patterns and their meanings, we can gain valuable insights into a person's thoughts, intentions, and level of engagement.

1. Saccades:

Saccades are rapid, jerky movements of the eyes as they shift focus from one point to another. These quick eye movements occur when we scan our surroundings or transition our gaze between objects or people. Saccades are essential for visual exploration and information gathering. They signify curiosity, alertness, and a desire to process visual stimuli.

For example, when someone is reading a book, their eyes move in saccades as they transition from one word to another, absorbing information.

2. Fixations:

Fixations refer to the moments when our eyes come to a pause and remain fixed on a specific object or point of interest. These still moments allow us to gather detailed information from our surroundings. Fixations are longer in duration compared to saccades and indicate focused attention and concentration.

During a conversation, fixations occur when we direct our gaze towards the person speaking or an object that captures our attention. It shows our interest and engagement in the subject matter.

3. Smooth Pursuit:

Smooth pursuit refers to the tracking movements our eyes make when following a moving object or person. It is a smooth and continuous motion that allows us to maintain visual contact with a target in motion.

Smooth pursuit eye movements indicate active involvement, curiosity, and the desire to maintain a connection with the subject of interest.

For example, when watching a tennis match, our eyes smoothly track the movement of the ball as it moves across the court.

4. Nystagmus:

Nystagmus is a condition characterized by involuntary and rapid eye movements, usually from side to side or up and down. While nystagmus can be a medical condition, it can also occur temporarily in response to certain stimuli or emotions. In non-verbal communication, nystagmus can indicate anxiety, nervousness, or discomfort.

For instance, during a high-pressure situation, such as public speaking, a person experiencing nystagmus may exhibit rapid eye movements due to heightened stress levels.

5. Eye Blocking:

Eye blocking refers to the act of covering or partially blocking the eyes with the hands, fingers, or other objects. This gesture can occur when someone is feeling uncomfortable, defensive, or attempting to shield themselves from a perceived threat or unwanted stimuli. Eye blocking can also signal skepticism, disagreement, or an attempt to hide emotions.

For example, if someone is asked a challenging question and they respond by covering their eyes or looking away, it may indicate they are feeling defensive or uncertain about their answer.

6. Rapid Eye Movement (REM):

REM refers to the quick and random movements of the eyes that occur during the rapid eye movement stage of sleep. However, in the context of non-verbal communication, rapid eye movements can occur during wakefulness and convey excitement, anticipation, or intense concentration.

For instance, when someone is passionately discussing a topic they are enthusiastic about, their eyes may exhibit rapid movements as they mentally process and express their thoughts.

Conclusion:

Eye movement patterns offer a fascinating insight into a person's mental and emotional state. By observing and interpreting these patterns, we can gain a deeper understanding of their engagement, attention, and emotional responses. Whether it's the rapid shifts of saccades, the focused fixations, or the smooth pursuit of a moving target, our eyes provide a rich tapestry of non-verbal cues. Paying attention to these eye movement patterns can enhance our communication skills, help us connect with others more effectively, and create a greater sense of understanding in our interactions.

Eye Signals in Different Situations

OUR EYES ARE NOT ONLY expressive but also serve as powerful signaling devices in various situations. In this chapter, we explore the intriguing realm of eye signals and their significance in different contexts. Whether it's in social interactions, professional environments, or personal relationships, understanding the subtle cues conveyed through eye signals can enhance our communication skills and deepen our understanding of others. Let's delve into the world of eye signals in different situations.

1. Social Interactions:

a) Interest and Attraction: When engaged in social interactions, eye signals can indicate interest and attraction. Dilated pupils, prolonged eye contact, and a gentle gaze can convey genuine curiosity and a desire to connect with the other person.

b) Disinterest or Boredom: Conversely, avoiding eye contact, frequent glancing around, or glazed eyes can signal disinterest or boredom. These eye signals suggest a lack of engagement or a desire to disengage from the conversation.

c) Deception or Dishonesty: Eye aversion, rapid blinking, or averted gaze can indicate deception or dishonesty. These eye signals may suggest that the person is uncomfortable with the truth or attempting to hide information.

2. Professional Environments:

a) Confidence and Assertiveness: Maintaining steady, direct eye contact in professional settings conveys confidence, assertiveness, and credibility. It demonstrates that you are attentive, composed, and in control of the situation.

b) Respect and Listening: Active listening in professional settings is often reflected through maintaining eye contact with the speaker. It conveys respect, professionalism, and a genuine interest in understanding and acknowledging the speaker's perspective.

c) Power Dynamics: Eye signals can also reflect power dynamics in professional environments. A dominant individual may employ intense eye contact and assertive gazes to establish authority, while a subordinate may exhibit more submissive eye contact to show deference or respect.

3. Personal Relationships:

a) Intimacy and Connection: Eye signals play a crucial role in intimate relationships. Deep, soulful gazes, gentle smiles, and shared glances can communicate love, connection, and emotional intimacy.

b) Trust and Honesty: Sustained eye contact, accompanied by open and honest expressions, fosters trust and transparency in personal relationships. It signifies a willingness to be vulnerable and creates a safe space for open communication.

c) Conflict and Tension: In moments of conflict or tension, eye signals can reveal underlying emotions. Avoiding eye contact, narrowed gaze, or intense stares may indicate anger, defensiveness, or resentment.

4. Public Speaking:

a) Engagement and Connection: Eye contact is paramount when delivering a speech or presentation. Maintaining eye contact with the audience demonstrates engagement, confidence, and the ability to connect with listeners on a personal level.

b) Non-Verbal Cues: Effective public speakers utilize eye signals to convey non-verbal cues. They may use subtle eye movements or glances to emphasize key points, establish a rapport with the audience, or engage specific individuals.

c) Calming Nerves: Engaging with friendly faces or making eye contact with supportive audience members can help calm nerves during public speaking. It provides a sense of connection and encouragement.

Conclusion:

Eye signals are an essential aspect of non-verbal communication in various situations. They serve as powerful indicators of interest, attraction, engagement, honesty, and power dynamics. By paying attention to these subtle cues, we can enhance our understanding of others, navigate social interactions, and build stronger connections. Whether it's in social, professional, or personal contexts, the language of the eyes adds depth and richness to our communication, allowing us to convey emotions, intentions, and establish meaningful connections with those around us.

Chapter 5: Interpreting Body Language Clusters

Body language is a complex and multi-dimensional form of non-verbal communication that conveys a wealth of information about a person's thoughts, emotions, and intentions. While individual body language cues provide valuable insights, it is the combination of multiple cues, known as body language clusters, that truly unlocks the intricate language of the body. In this chapter, we explore the art of interpreting body language clusters and unravel the hidden messages they hold. By understanding how different body language cues interact and reinforce each other, we can gain a more accurate understanding of a person's underlying sentiments and decode their unspoken communication.

The Power of Body Language Clusters:

Just as words gain meaning through their arrangement in sentences and paragraphs, body language cues gain significance when they form cohesive clusters. A single gesture or expression may have multiple interpretations, but when combined with other complementary cues, it paints a more comprehensive picture. Body language clusters provide context, nuance, and a deeper understanding of the speaker's true feelings and intentions.

Combining Multiple Cues for Accurate Readings

INTERPRETING BODY LANGUAGE is a fascinating endeavor that involves understanding the subtle cues and non-verbal signals people emit. While individual body language cues offer valuable insights, combining multiple cues is the key to achieving accurate readings and gaining a deeper understanding of a person's true intentions. In this chapter, we explore the art of combining multiple cues in body language analysis and provide examples that illustrate how different cues work together to create a comprehensive picture.

The Power of Combining Cues:

When it comes to body language, no single cue should be taken in isolation. Combining multiple cues allows us to cross-reference and validate the signals being conveyed. By considering the interplay of gestures, expressions, postures, and other non-verbal cues, we can achieve more accurate interpretations and uncover the underlying messages hidden within the body language.

Examples of Combining Multiple Cues:

1. Example: Nervousness and Deception

Imagine a person is giving a presentation and displays a combination of cues. They may have a fast heartbeat (evidenced by a pulsating neck vein), a shaky voice, excessive sweating, and fidgeting hands. While each cue individually suggests nervousness, when combined, they may also indicate potential deception. The person's anxiety might stem from their attempt to conceal the truth or from the fear of being discovered.

2. Example: Confidence and Openness

Consider a scenario where someone displays a cluster of cues that exude confidence and openness. They stand tall with good posture, maintain steady eye contact, have relaxed facial expressions, and open gestures (such as arms apart and palms facing upward). This combination of cues signals self-assurance, approachability, and a genuine willingness to engage in conversation or interaction.

3. Example: Discomfort and Disagreement

In a group discussion, an individual might exhibit cues indicating discomfort and disagreement. They could display crossed arms, lean away from the conversation, furrowed brows, and frequent glances towards the exit. This combination of cues suggests their disagreement with the discussed topic or their discomfort with the conversation's direction.

4. Example: Interest and Engagement

Imagine observing someone who demonstrates a combination of cues indicating interest and engagement. They lean forward with an open posture, maintain direct eye contact, nod in agreement, and display occasional smiles or subtle head tilts. These cues collectively convey their genuine interest in the conversation, active listening, and a desire to connect with the speaker.

5. Example: Dominance and Authority

In a leadership context, someone may exhibit cues that signal dominance and authority. They might employ a strong, upright posture, maintain direct and prolonged eye contact, use expansive gestures, and speak in a confident and assertive tone. This combination of cues establishes their position of power and asserts their authority within the group or organizational hierarchy.

Conclusion:

Combining multiple cues in body language analysis is essential for achieving accurate readings and understanding the complex messages conveyed through non-verbal communication. By considering how different cues interact and support each other, we can gain deeper insights into a person's thoughts, emotions, and intentions. Examples such as nervousness and deception, confidence and openness, discomfort and disagreement, interest and engagement, and dominance and authority illustrate the power of combining cues for more accurate interpretations. By honing our ability to observe and integrate these cues, we can enhance our overall proficiency in reading body language, strengthening our interpersonal skills, and fostering better connections with others.

Recognizing Congruence and Incongruence

IN THE INTRICATE REALM of body language, one of the key skills to develop is the ability to recognize congruence and incongruence between verbal and non-verbal cues. Congruence occurs when a person's words align harmoniously with their body language, reinforcing the intended message. Incongruence, on the other hand, arises when there is a mismatch between what is said and what is non-verbally expressed. In this chapter, we delve into the art of recognizing congruence and incongruence, exploring the subtle nuances that can provide valuable insights into a person's true thoughts, feelings, and intentions.

Understanding Congruence:

Congruence refers to the alignment between a person's verbal and non-verbal cues. When verbal and non-verbal messages are congruent, they create a powerful sense of authenticity, trust, and transparency. Observing congruent cues allows us to accurately interpret the speaker's intended meaning and enhances our ability to connect and communicate effectively.

1. Verbal and Non-Verbal Alignment: Recognizing congruence involves observing how a person's words and their accompanying non-verbal cues align. For example, if someone expresses excitement while their face lights up with a genuine smile and their body becomes animated, it signifies congruence between their verbal expression and non-verbal cues.

2. Emotional Consistency: Congruence extends to the emotional realm as well. When a person's emotional state matches their words and non-verbal cues, it reinforces the credibility and authenticity of their message. For instance, if someone shares a story about a tragic event with a somber tone, teary eyes, and a downcast posture, it reflects emotional congruence.

Recognizing Incongruence:

Incongruence occurs when there is a disconnect between verbal and non-verbal cues. It is essential to recognize incongruence, as it often signals hidden emotions, concealed intentions, or a lack of sincerity in communication. By identifying these inconsistencies, we can gain a deeper understanding of the speaker's underlying thoughts and motivations.

1. Mixed Messages: Incongruence can arise when a person's words and non-verbal cues convey conflicting messages. For instance, if someone claims to be excited about an opportunity but exhibits tense body language, lack of eye contact, and a subdued tone, it suggests a discrepancy between their verbal expression and true feelings.

2. Microexpressions: Microexpressions are fleeting facial expressions that reveal true emotions. They can be a powerful indicator of incongruence. For example, if someone smiles politely while their microexpression momentarily displays signs of sadness or anger, it suggests concealed emotions that contradict their verbal communication.

3. Incongruent Body Language: Incongruence can also manifest in specific body language cues. For instance, crossed arms, fidgeting, or avoiding eye contact while expressing agreement or positivity may indicate an underlying disagreement or discomfort.

Importance of Congruence and Incongruence:

Recognizing congruence and incongruence in body language is crucial for gaining deeper insights into a person's true thoughts, feelings, and intentions. It enables us to discern hidden emotions, identify potential deception, and navigate interpersonal interactions with greater awareness and sensitivity. By honing our ability to recognize these nuances, we can enhance our communication skills, establish stronger connections, and foster trust and understanding in our relationships.

Conclusion:

Recognizing congruence and incongruence in body language is an invaluable skill that allows us to decipher the true meaning behind a person's verbal and non-verbal cues. By observing the alignment or mismatch between what is said and what is expressed non-verbally, we gain profound insights into a person's authenticity, emotional state, and sincerity. Understanding congruence and incongruence enhances our ability to connect, communicate effectively, and navigate social interactions with heightened awareness. By cultivating this skill, we become adept at deciphering the intricate language of the body and unlocking the hidden messages it conveys.

Body Language in Specific Contexts

BODY LANGUAGE PLAYS a pivotal role in our interactions across various contexts, and understanding its significance in specific situations can greatly influence our success and effectiveness. In this chapter, we delve into the nuances of body language within specific contexts such as job interviews, negotiations, and other professional settings. By exploring the unique dynamics and expectations of each context, we can harness the power of body language to make a positive impression, convey confidence, and build rapport with others.

1. Job Interviews:

Job interviews are critical moments where first impressions and non-verbal cues carry substantial weight. Understanding how to navigate the body language expectations in job interviews can significantly impact your chances of success.

a) Posture and Poise: Sitting or standing with an upright posture conveys confidence and professionalism. Avoid slouching, as it can project disinterest or a lack of confidence.

b) Eye Contact: Maintain good eye contact to establish trust and demonstrate active engagement. However, be mindful not to make it overly intense or uncomfortable.

c) Hand Gestures: Use natural and purposeful hand gestures to emphasize key points and convey enthusiasm. However, be cautious of excessive or distracting movements that may overshadow your message.

d) Facial Expressions: Display genuine smiles, attentive expressions, and appropriate facial reactions to demonstrate interest and positivity. This helps build rapport and establishes a connection with the interviewer.

2. Negotiations:

Negotiations involve a delicate dance of power, persuasion, and influence. Understanding the subtleties of body language can give you an edge in achieving successful outcomes.

a) Assertive Body Language: Project confidence and assertiveness through open body postures, expansive gestures, and steady eye contact. This conveys conviction and signals that you stand firm in your position.

b) Mirroring and Matching: Mirroring and matching the body language of the other party can foster rapport and create a sense of alignment. However, do so subtly and naturally to avoid appearing contrived or manipulative.

c) Listening Cues: Demonstrate active listening by nodding, maintaining eye contact, and using appropriate facial expressions. This conveys that you value the other party's input and encourages open communication.

d) Control of Nervous Cues: Keep nervous cues in check, such as fidgeting or repetitive movements. Practice techniques like deep breathing and maintaining a calm demeanor to project confidence and composure.

3. Presentations and Public Speaking:

Effective body language is crucial when delivering presentations or engaging in public speaking engagements. It helps captivate the audience and enhances the impact of your message.

a) Posture and Stance: Stand tall with an open and confident posture, allowing for natural gestures that support your message. This projects authority and credibility.

b) Movement and Gestures: Utilize purposeful movements and gestures to enhance your presentation. Move with intention and use gestures that align with your words, emphasizing key points and creating visual interest.

c) Vocal Variety and Expression: Combine body language with vocal variety to engage your audience. Modulate your voice, use appropriate pauses, and synchronize your body movements with the rhythm of your speech.

d) Audience Engagement: Establish a connection with the audience through eye contact, including individuals across the room. This helps create a sense of connection and involvement.

Conclusion:

Understanding body language within specific contexts empowers us to navigate professional situations with confidence and finesse. Whether in job interviews, negotiations, or public speaking engagements, the appropriate use of body language enhances our ability to make a positive impact, build rapport, and effectively communicate our message. By harnessing the power of body language in these contexts, we position ourselves for success and create meaningful connections that contribute to our personal and professional growth.

Chapter 6:. Adapting Your Body Language

Adapting one's body language is a skill that allows us to effectively communicate and connect with a wide range of individuals and navigate diverse social situations. In this chapter, we explore the importance of adapting body language and how it can foster understanding, empathy, and harmonious interactions. By understanding the principles and techniques of adapting body language, we can bridge communication gaps, build rapport, and cultivate meaningful relationships across various cultural, professional, and personal contexts.

The Power of Adaptation:

Every person we encounter is unique, with different cultural backgrounds, communication styles, and preferences. Adapting our body language helps us meet others where they are and create a more comfortable and inclusive environment for effective communication. By recognizing and responding to the cues and needs of others, we demonstrate respect, empathy, and the willingness to connect on their terms.

Projecting Confidence through Body Language

ADAPTING ONE'S BODY language is a skill that allows us to effectively communicate and connect with a wide range of individuals and navigate diverse social situations. In this chapter, we explore the importance of adapting body language and how it can foster understanding, empathy, and harmonious interactions. By understanding the principles and techniques of adapting body language, we can bridge communication gaps, build rapport, and cultivate meaningful relationships across various cultural, professional, and personal contexts.

The Power of Adaptation:

Every person we encounter is unique, with different cultural backgrounds, communication styles, and preferences. Adapting our body language helps us meet others where they are and create a more comfortable and inclusive environment for effective communication. By recognizing and responding to the cues and needs of others, we demonstrate respect, empathy, and the willingness to connect on their terms.

Adapting to Cultural Differences:

Cultural variations significantly impact body language norms and interpretations. What may be considered acceptable or respectful in one culture might be perceived differently in another. Adapting our body language to align with cultural norms fosters mutual understanding and avoids misunderstandings or unintended offenses.

Adapting to Professional Settings:

Body language plays a crucial role in professional settings, where impressions, credibility, and professionalism are paramount. Adapting our body language in these contexts allows us to project competence, confidence, and professionalism. Whether in job interviews, business meetings, or networking events, understanding and aligning with professional body language expectations contribute to successful outcomes and positive relationships.

Adapting to Personal Relationships:

Our body language influences our interactions with friends, family, and romantic partners. Adapting our body language in personal relationships enables us to express empathy, support, and affection effectively. By being attuned to the needs and preferences of our loved ones, we create an environment of understanding and strengthen the emotional bonds that underpin healthy relationships.

Techniques for Adapting Body Language:

1. Observation and Awareness: Cultivate the skill of keen observation to pick up on non-verbal cues and body language signals from others. Be aware of your own body language and how it may be perceived by different individuals or in various contexts.

2. Mirroring and Matching: Mirroring and matching the body language of others can help establish rapport and foster a sense of connection. However, exercise caution to do so subtly and authentically, avoiding mimicry or appearing insincere.

3. Flexibility and Openness: Be open to adjusting your body language to accommodate the preferences and comfort levels of others. Flexibility allows for smoother interactions and demonstrates respect for individual differences.

4. Sensitivity to Cultural Context: Educate yourself about the body language norms and customs of different cultures to navigate cross-cultural interactions with sensitivity and avoid unintentional offense.

Conclusion:

Adapting our body language is a powerful tool for effective communication, understanding, and building relationships. By recognizing the diverse needs and preferences of others, we can adjust our body language to create a welcoming and inclusive atmosphere. Whether in cultural contexts, professional settings, or personal relationships, adapting our body language demonstrates empathy, respect, and a genuine desire to connect. By honing the skill of adapting body language, we become more adept at fostering positive interactions, bridging gaps in communication, and creating harmonious connections with the diverse individuals we encounter in our lives.

Building Rapport with Mirroring and Matching

BUILDING RAPPORT IS a fundamental aspect of effective communication and establishing connections with others. One powerful technique for building rapport is mirroring and matching, which involves subtly aligning our body language, speech patterns, and behaviors with those of the person we're interacting with. In this chapter, we explore the art of mirroring and matching and how it can foster rapport, trust, and understanding. By mastering this technique, we can create harmonious relationships, enhance communication, and deepen our connections with others.

Understanding Mirroring and Matching:

Mirroring and matching involve subtly imitating or synchronizing our behavior with someone else's in a natural and non-intrusive way. This technique taps into our innate human tendency to connect with others and establishes a sense of familiarity and similarity. By mirroring and matching, we create a subconscious bond, making others feel comfortable and increasing the likelihood of positive interactions.

1. Body Language Mirroring:

Mirroring body language involves subtly imitating the other person's postures, gestures, and movements. By observing their body language and mirroring it in a genuine and subtle manner, we establish a sense of rapport and create a non-verbal connection.

a) Posture and Position: Observe the person's posture and adopt a similar one. If they lean forward, you can lean forward slightly as well. If they cross their legs, you can do the same. This mirroring creates a sense of alignment and engagement.

b) Gestures and Movements: Notice the person's gestures and replicate them naturally. If they use their hands to express themselves, you can incorporate similar gestures in your own communication. Be mindful of mirroring without appearing forced or mimicking excessively.

c) Facial Expressions: Pay attention to the person's facial expressions and mirror them subtly. If they smile, respond with a genuine smile. Mirror their expressions of interest, concern, or surprise to establish a deeper connection.

2. Vocal Mirroring:

Matching the vocal aspects of communication helps create a sense of resonance and familiarity, enhancing rapport and understanding.

a) Tone and Pitch: Observe the person's tone and pitch of voice and adjust yours accordingly. If they speak softly and calmly, you can match their tone. If they speak with energy and enthusiasm, you can reflect that in your own voice.

b) Pace and Rhythm: Adapt your speaking pace to match theirs. If they speak slowly and deliberately, you can adjust your pace accordingly. Similarly, if they have a faster pace, you can synchronize your speech to maintain a comfortable rhythm.

c) Speech Patterns and Vocabulary: Notice the person's speech patterns, phrases, and choice of words. Incorporate similar language patterns naturally into your conversation, reflecting their style and preferences.

3. Energy and Emotions:

Matching the energy level and emotional state of the other person can create a deeper connection and rapport.

a) Energy Level: Observe the person's energy level, whether they are calm and composed or enthusiastic and energetic. Adapt your own energy level to align with theirs, creating a balanced and harmonious interaction.

b) Emotional State: Pay attention to the person's emotional cues and respond empathetically. If they express excitement or happiness, reflect those emotions genuinely. Likewise, if they are discussing something serious or sad, adjust your demeanor to show understanding and empathy.

Benefits and Considerations:

Building rapport through mirroring and matching has numerous benefits, such as establishing trust, creating a comfortable environment, and fostering effective communication. However, it's important to practice mirroring and matching with authenticity and respect for individual differences.

a) Authenticity: Mirroring and matching should be done subtly and naturally, without coming across as imitation or manipulation. Focus on genuine connection rather than mimicry.

b) Respect for Differences: Not

everyone responds to mirroring and matching in the same way. Be mindful of cultural norms, personal boundaries, and the comfort level of the other person. Adapt your mirroring to align with their preferences and communication style.

c) Active Listening: Mirroring and matching go hand in hand with active listening. Pay close attention to the other person's non-verbal cues, speech patterns, and emotional states. This level of attentiveness helps you respond appropriately and build a stronger rapport.

Conclusion:

Mirroring and matching are powerful techniques for building rapport and establishing connections with others. By aligning our body language, speech patterns, and energy with those of the person we're interacting with, we create a sense of familiarity, trust, and understanding. Remember, mirroring and matching should be done authentically, with respect for individual differences. When employed effectively, this technique enhances communication, deepens relationships, and paves the way for more meaningful and harmonious connections with others.

Chapter 7: Body Language Pitfalls to Avoid

While body language is a valuable tool for communication, it is essential to be aware of certain pitfalls that can hinder our ability to convey our intended messages effectively. In this chapter, we explore the common body language pitfalls to avoid, as they can lead to misunderstandings, misinterpretations, and even damaged relationships. By understanding and addressing these pitfalls, we can enhance our non-verbal communication skills, ensure clarity, and strengthen the positive impact of our body language.

Common Mistakes and Misinterpretations in Body Language

DESPITE THE IMPORTANCE of body language in communication, it is susceptible to various mistakes and misinterpretations that can hinder effective understanding and lead to misunderstandings. In this chapter, we explore common mistakes and misinterpretations in body language, shedding light on the potential pitfalls that can arise. By understanding these pitfalls and learning how to navigate them, we can improve our ability to accurately interpret and respond to non-verbal cues, fostering better communication and stronger connections with others.

1. Crossed Arms:

Mistake: Crossed arms are often associated with defensiveness or resistance. However, this gesture can also be a result of feeling cold, tired, or simply seeking comfort.

Interpretation: It is essential not to jump to conclusions based solely on crossed arms. Consider the context, the person's overall body language, and other cues to determine the true meaning. They may be open to conversation despite the crossed arms.

Example: Sarah crossed her arms during the meeting, which made her colleagues assume she was opposed to the idea. However, upon further discussion, they realized she was feeling chilly due to the air conditioning.

2. Lack of Eye Contact:

Mistake: Not maintaining eye contact is often perceived as disinterest or dishonesty. However, cultural differences, shyness, or personal preferences can also influence eye contact behavior.

Interpretation: It is crucial to consider individual and cultural factors when interpreting eye contact. Some individuals may find direct eye contact uncomfortable or may have been taught to avoid prolonged eye contact as a sign of respect.

Example: During a conversation, John avoided direct eye contact, leading his colleague to think he was being untrustworthy. In reality, John's cultural background placed less emphasis on eye contact, and he was actively listening and engaging in the conversation.

3. Nervous Gestures:

Mistake: Nervous gestures, such as fidgeting, tapping fingers, or playing with objects, are often perceived as signs of anxiety or dishonesty. However, they can also be expressions of excitement or anticipation.

Interpretation: It is essential to consider the overall context and the person's demeanor before drawing conclusions about nervous gestures. These behaviors can be manifestations of various emotions, and making assumptions solely based on them can lead to misunderstandings.

Example: Samantha noticed her interviewee fidgeting with a pen and assumed he was unprepared. However, after further observation, she realized he was merely excited about the opportunity and trying to channel his energy.

4. Personal Space Violation:

Mistake: Invading someone's personal space can be seen as aggressive or disrespectful. However, cultural differences, individual preferences, or crowded environments can influence the perception of personal space.

Interpretation: Respect personal boundaries and be aware that different cultures have varying notions of personal space. Always gauge the other person's comfort level and adapt accordingly.

Example: Mike stood closer to his coworker than usual, assuming a friendly rapport. However, his coworker felt uncomfortable because she preferred a larger personal space. Understanding personal boundaries is crucial for maintaining positive interactions.

5. Facial Expressions Misread:

Mistake: Facial expressions can be misinterpreted if observed in isolation or without considering the context. Smiling, for example, can indicate friendliness, but it can also mask discomfort or conceal negative emotions.

Interpretation: Pay attention to the overall facial expressions, body language, and verbal cues to accurately understand a person's emotional state. Contextual clues are essential for interpreting facial expressions correctly.

Example: Chris assumed that Lisa's smile meant she agreed with his proposal. However, during the discussion, Lisa's facial expressions suggested she had reservations. By considering the broader context, Chris realized that Lisa's

smile was a polite gesture rather than genuine agreement.

Conclusion:

Understanding and navigating common mistakes and misinterpretations in body language is crucial for effective communication. By recognizing that certain gestures or expressions can have multiple meanings, we can avoid making hasty judgments and instead engage in open and non-judgmental communication. Remember to consider the context, individual differences, and cultural factors when interpreting body language. By doing so, we can foster better understanding, strengthen relationships, and build a foundation of trust and rapport in our interactions with others.

Overcoming Nervous Tics and Subconscious Gestures

NERVOUS TICS AND SUBCONSCIOUS gestures are common occurrences when we experience anxiety, stress, or discomfort in various social or professional situations. These involuntary movements or habits can inadvertently send unintended signals to others, potentially affecting our credibility, confidence, and overall communication effectiveness. In this chapter, we explore strategies and techniques for overcoming nervous tics and subconscious gestures, allowing us to project a more composed and self-assured demeanor in our interactions.

1. Awareness:

The first step in overcoming nervous tics and subconscious gestures is developing self-awareness. Pay close attention to your body language and identify any repetitive or unconscious movements that tend to manifest during moments of anxiety or stress. It could be finger tapping, hair twirling, foot shaking, or any other physical gesture.

2. Breathing and Relaxation Techniques:

Deep breathing exercises and relaxation techniques can help alleviate anxiety and reduce the likelihood of nervous tics. Practice diaphragmatic breathing, where you breathe deeply into your abdomen, to promote a sense of calmness and relaxation. Incorporate regular mindfulness or meditation practices into your routine to enhance overall self-awareness and manage stress levels effectively.

3. Positive Visualization and Mental Preparation:

Visualize yourself in situations where you typically experience nervous tics or subconscious gestures. Imagine yourself remaining calm, composed, and in control. Visualizing positive outcomes and mentally rehearsing confident body language can help reprogram your subconscious mind and reduce anxiety-triggered movements.

4. Physical Exercises and Stress Management:

Engaging in regular physical exercise not only improves your overall well-being but also helps manage stress and anxiety. Incorporate activities such as yoga, Pilates, or martial arts into your routine, as they promote body awareness, balance, and control. Additionally, consider stress management techniques such as journaling, engaging in hobbies, or seeking professional support if needed.

5. Practice in Low-Stress Environments:

Gradually expose yourself to situations that trigger nervous tics or subconscious gestures in low-stress environments. Practice maintaining composed body language and consciously suppressing any unwanted movements. As you become more comfortable and confident, gradually increase the level of challenge by exposing yourself to slightly more stressful situations.

6. Seek Feedback and Support:

Ask trusted friends, family members, or mentors for feedback on your body language and any noticeable nervous tics or subconscious gestures. They can provide valuable insight and help identify specific habits that you may not be aware of. Consider working with a communication coach or therapist who specializes in non-verbal communication to receive personalized guidance and support.

7. Replacing Habits with Positive Alternatives:

Identify alternative, positive behaviors to replace your nervous tics or subconscious gestures. For example, if you tend to fidget with your hands, consciously choose to clasp them together or place them calmly on your lap. Channel nervous energy into purposeful gestures that convey confidence and control, such as purposeful hand gestures during a presentation.

Conclusion:

Overcoming nervous tics and subconscious gestures requires self-awareness, practice, and patience. By implementing the strategies outlined in this chapter, you can gradually gain control over your body language and project a more confident and composed image. Remember that it is normal to experience moments of anxiety or stress, but by actively addressing and managing your body language, you can effectively communicate your intended messages and enhance your overall presence in various social and professional settings.

Ethical Considerations in Reading and Using Body Language

WHEN DELVING INTO THE realm of body language, it is crucial to acknowledge and address the ethical considerations associated with its interpretation and use. As body language can reveal personal and emotional states, it is essential to approach its analysis with sensitivity, respect, and awareness of potential biases. In this chapter, we explore the ethical considerations in reading and using body language, emphasizing the importance of responsible and mindful application to ensure the integrity of interpersonal interactions.

1. Respect for Privacy and Consent:

Respecting privacy and obtaining consent is paramount when reading and interpreting someone's body language. Understand that body language can reveal intimate emotions and vulnerabilities. Always seek explicit consent when analyzing or discussing another person's non-verbal cues, ensuring their comfort and trust in the process.

2. Avoiding Stereotyping and Generalizations:

Body language varies across individuals, cultures, and contexts. It is crucial to avoid stereotyping or making generalizations based on someone's body language. Recognize that non-verbal cues are influenced by a myriad of factors, including cultural backgrounds, personality traits, and individual experiences. Treat each person as a unique individual and refrain from making assumptions solely based on their body language.

3. Non-Verbal Cues as Supplementary, Not Definitive:

While body language provides valuable insights into a person's emotions and thoughts, it should not be considered as the sole basis for judgments or conclusions. Non-verbal cues should be used in conjunction with verbal communication and other contextual factors to form a more comprehensive understanding. Relying solely on body language can lead to misinterpretations and misunderstandings.

4. Awareness of Bias and Cultural Differences:

Recognize and address your own biases and preconceptions when interpreting body language. Be aware of the influence of cultural norms, as interpretations of body language can vary significantly across different cultures. Seek to understand and educate yourself about cultural differences to avoid misjudgments and ensure a more accurate interpretation of non-verbal cues.

5. Confidentiality and Professional Boundaries:

If you are in a professional setting where body language analysis is part of your role (e.g., therapist, mediator, or coach), it is essential to maintain confidentiality and respect professional boundaries. Handle the information obtained from body language with discretion and ensure it is used solely for the intended purpose of helping and supporting the individual.

6. Contextual Considerations:

Consider the broader context when interpreting body language. Recognize that certain non-verbal cues may have different meanings depending on the situation. Take into account the environment, the relationship between individuals, and the specific circumstances to avoid misinterpretation or overgeneralization.

Conclusion:

Ethical considerations play a significant role in reading and using body language. It is essential to approach the interpretation of non-verbal cues with respect, sensitivity, and cultural awareness. By maintaining privacy, obtaining consent, avoiding stereotypes, and recognizing the limitations of body language, we can ensure that our interpretations and applications are responsible, accurate, and mindful. Upholding ethical standards in the realm of body language not only promotes understanding and connection but also preserves the integrity of interpersonal interactions and respects the dignity of others.

Chapter 8: Body Language in Relationships

Body language plays a fundamental role in our interpersonal relationships, as it often conveys unspoken messages that can enhance or hinder the dynamics between individuals. Whether it's a romantic partnership, friendship, or familial bond, understanding and effectively using body language can significantly impact the quality and depth of our connections. In this chapter, we explore the importance of body language in relationships and how it influences our interactions, emotions, and overall relational satisfaction.

1. The Silent Language of Relationships:

While verbal communication forms the basis of our conversations, the silent language of body cues and gestures can convey emotions, intentions, and desires that words alone cannot fully express. Body language provides subtle clues about a person's comfort, trust, and attraction, allowing us to navigate and understand the unspoken aspects of our relationships.

2. Non-Verbal Communication as a Mirror:

Body language acts as a mirror, reflecting our internal state and emotions to those around us. It offers insights into our level of engagement, openness, and emotional well-being. Similarly, it provides valuable feedback to our partners, helping them gauge our reactions, needs, and responses. Understanding and interpreting these non-verbal cues can foster empathy, deepen understanding, and facilitate effective communication in relationships.

3. Enhancing Emotional Intimacy:

Body language plays a vital role in cultivating emotional intimacy within relationships. The way we physically connect, such as through hugs, cuddling, or holding hands, conveys warmth, support, and a sense of closeness. Eye contact, facial expressions, and touch all contribute to the emotional bond we share with others. Being attuned to these non-verbal cues helps foster emotional safety, trust, and a deeper connection with our loved ones.

4. Resolving Conflict and Building Trust:

During conflicts or disagreements, body language often takes center stage, revealing underlying emotions and attitudes. Defensive postures, crossed arms, or avoidance of eye contact can signal defensiveness or withdrawal. On the other hand, open and relaxed body language, active listening, and non-threatening gestures can foster understanding, empathy, and trust during challenging conversations. Being mindful of our own body language and reading our partner's cues can facilitate more constructive conflict resolution and strengthen the foundation of trust in relationships.

5. Unspoken Messages of Attraction:

Body language plays a crucial role in romantic relationships, especially during the initial stages of attraction. Subtle cues such as leaning in, mirroring each other's movements, playful touches, and prolonged eye contact can communicate interest, chemistry, and desire. Being attuned to these signals can enhance the romantic connection and deepen the bond between partners.

6. Cultural Variations and Individual Differences:

It is important to acknowledge that body language is influenced by cultural norms and individual differences. Different cultures have distinct gestures, personal space boundaries, and rules surrounding touch. Additionally, each individual has their unique body language preferences and comfort zones. Respect for cultural diversity and understanding individual differences contribute to effective communication and harmony in relationships.

Conclusion:

Body language serves as a powerful tool in our relationships, influencing the depth of emotional connection, trust, and overall satisfaction. By being mindful of our own non-verbal cues and attuned to those of our partners, we can enhance our communication, foster empathy, resolve conflicts more effectively, and deepen the bonds we share. Body language provides a profound avenue for emotional expression, connection, and understanding, enriching our relationships and nurturing the connections that truly matter.

Understanding Romantic Body Language

ROMANTIC RELATIONSHIPS are characterized by a unique set of non-verbal cues and gestures that convey attraction, desire, and emotional connection. Understanding and interpreting romantic body language can provide valuable insights into the dynamics of a relationship, the level of interest, and the depth of emotional intimacy. In this chapter, we explore various aspects of romantic body language, providing examples and explanations to enhance your understanding of this subtle yet powerful form of communication.

1. Proximity and Personal Space:

In romantic relationships, proximity plays a significant role in expressing intimacy and attraction. Couples often display a desire to be physically close to each other. They may stand or sit in close proximity, leaning towards one another, or engaging in gentle touches. The desire for physical closeness is evident in actions such as reaching for each other's hands, resting heads on shoulders, or intertwining fingers. For example, when a couple sits side by side on a bench, their bodies naturally lean towards each other, indicating their desire for connection and closeness.

2. Eye Contact and Gaze:

Eye contact is a powerful tool in romantic relationships, capable of conveying a range of emotions and intentions. Prolonged eye contact, particularly with dilated pupils, signals interest, attraction, and a desire for deeper connection. Couples in love often engage in lingering gazes, looking into each other's eyes with intensity and warmth. For instance, when sharing a romantic dinner, partners may maintain eye contact while smiling, creating a deep sense of emotional connection and affection.

3. Touch and Affection:

Touch is a vital component of romantic body language, serving as a means of physical connection and emotional expression. Couples engaged in a romantic relationship frequently engage in affectionate touch, such as holding hands, hugging, or gentle caresses. These touches can be both spontaneous and intentional, serving to reinforce emotional bonds and convey love and care. A couple strolling in a park might interlace their fingers as they walk, symbolizing their emotional and physical connection.

4. Mirroring and Synchronization:

Mirroring is a phenomenon commonly observed in romantic relationships, where partners unconsciously mimic each other's body language, gestures, and even speech patterns. It is a sign of rapport, emotional connection, and compatibility. For instance, partners sitting across from each other in a café may unknowingly mirror each other's hand gestures or adopt similar postures, signifying their harmonious connection and shared understanding.

5. Facial Expressions:

Facial expressions are powerful indicators of emotional states and attraction. In romantic relationships, partners often exhibit genuine smiles, also known as Duchenne smiles, which involve the contraction of both the mouth and the eyes. These smiles convey warmth, happiness, and genuine affection. Raised eyebrows, fluttering eyelashes, and a softening of facial features are additional subtle cues that indicate attraction and interest. For example, when a partner sees their significant other after a long day, their face might light up with a wide, genuine smile, reflecting their joy and love.

6. Vocal Cues and Tone of Voice:

Romantic body language extends beyond physical gestures to include vocal cues and tone of voice. In intimate relationships, partners often adopt a softer tone, speak in hushed voices, or use endearing nicknames. These verbal cues contribute to a sense of emotional closeness and intimacy. For instance, when partners share a private moment, they might speak softly, using words of affection like "sweetheart" or "darling," creating a warm and tender atmosphere.

Conclusion:

Understanding romantic body language can deepen your comprehension of the dynamics and emotional connection within a relationship. By paying attention to proximity, eye contact, touch, facial expressions, vocal cues, and mirroring, you can gain valuable insights into the level of attraction, emotional intimacy, and overall satisfaction between partners. Remember that body language is context-dependent and varies across individuals and cultures, so it is important to consider these factors when interpreting romantic non-verbal cues. Developing sensitivity to these subtle signals will allow you to enhance your communication, strengthen your connection, and foster a deeper bond with your romantic partner.

Non-Verbal Cues in Friendships and Social Connections

NON-VERBAL CUES PLAY a significant role in our friendships and social interactions, shaping the dynamics, trust, and depth of connections we share with others. In this chapter, we explore the importance of non-verbal communication in friendships and social connections, highlighting the various cues and gestures that contribute to understanding, bonding, and maintaining healthy relationships.

1. Body Language and Approachability:

Approachability is crucial in forming new friendships and fostering social connections. Open and inviting body language signals a willingness to engage with others. It includes uncrossed arms, relaxed posture, maintaining eye contact, and a warm smile. These cues communicate that you are receptive and interested in connecting with others, making it easier for potential friends to approach and initiate conversations.

2. Active Listening and Engagement:

Active listening is an essential component of effective communication in friendships. Non-verbal cues, such as nodding, maintaining eye contact, and facing the speaker, indicate attentiveness and genuine interest. These signals show that you value their words and are fully present in the conversation. Additionally, leaning in slightly, mirroring the speaker's gestures, and providing verbal and non-verbal feedback contribute to active engagement and demonstrate your investment in the interaction.

3. Gestures of Support and Comfort:

In friendships, non-verbal cues can convey support, empathy, and comfort. Physical gestures, such as a reassuring pat on the back or a comforting hug, can provide solace during difficult times. Facial expressions, like a compassionate smile or a furrowed brow, show empathy and understanding. These non-verbal signals communicate that you are there for your friends, ready to offer support and lend a listening ear when needed.

4. Shared Non-Verbal Language:

Close friendships often develop their own shared non-verbal language or inside jokes, consisting of unique gestures, facial expressions, or references understood only by the involved parties. These cues serve as a form of bonding and strengthen the connection between friends. For example, a simple glance or a particular hand gesture can instantly convey a message or evoke shared memories, deepening the bond and sense of belonging within the friendship.

5. Respect for Personal Boundaries:

Respecting personal boundaries is vital in maintaining healthy friendships. Non-verbal cues, such as respecting personal space and body language, indicate an understanding of the other person's comfort zone. Being mindful of cues that suggest discomfort, like leaning away or avoiding physical contact, is essential. It is important to give friends their desired space and allow them to express their boundaries freely, promoting a sense of safety and trust within the friendship.

6. Emotional Expressions:

Non-verbal cues are instrumental in expressing and interpreting emotions within friendships. Facial expressions, such as smiles, laughter, or furrowed brows, provide immediate insight into a friend's emotional state. Non-verbal cues can also indicate enthusiasm, excitement, or sadness. For instance, a friend's widened eyes and animated gestures might signify their excitement about sharing good news or their slumped posture and subdued voice could indicate their need for support during difficult times.

Conclusion:

Non-verbal cues play a vital role in friendships and social connections. From approachability and active listening to gestures of support, shared non-verbal language, and respecting personal boundaries, these cues contribute to the overall understanding, trust, and emotional connection within friendships. By being aware of and effectively utilizing non-verbal communication, you can foster deeper bonds, enhance mutual understanding, and nurture fulfilling friendships and social connections that bring joy and support to your life.

Body Language in Family Dynamics

BODY LANGUAGE IS A powerful form of non-verbal communication that significantly impacts family dynamics. Within the context of familial relationships, understanding and interpreting body language cues can provide insights into emotions, intentions, and the overall health of the family unit. In this chapter, we explore the significance of body language in family dynamics and how it influences communication, connection, and the overall well-being of family relationships.

1. Parent-Child Bonding:

Body language plays a crucial role in establishing and nurturing the parent-child bond. Infants and young children rely heavily on non-verbal cues to understand and connect with their parents. Gentle touches, eye contact, and comforting body language convey a sense of security and love. For example, a parent cradling their child in their arms, making eye contact, and gently rocking them signifies affection and provides a sense of safety and attachment.

2. Sibling Interactions:

Body language also influences sibling interactions within a family. Siblings may engage in playful gestures, mirroring each other's movements, or teasing through non-verbal cues. These interactions contribute to the development of social skills, empathy, and cooperation. For instance, siblings engaged in a playful wrestling match might use exaggerated facial expressions and body movements to convey their enjoyment and create a sense of camaraderie.

3. Expressing Love and Affection:

Non-verbal cues are instrumental in expressing love and affection within family relationships. Hugs, kisses, and physical embraces convey warmth, acceptance, and emotional connection. A gentle pat on the back or a loving gaze can communicate care and support. For example, a parent embracing their child after a long day at school or a sibling offering a comforting hug to a sibling going through a difficult time exemplify the expression of love and support through non-verbal cues.

4. Conflict Resolution:

Body language plays a significant role in conflict resolution within families. Non-verbal cues can either escalate or de-escalate tensions during disagreements. Defensive postures, crossed arms, and avoiding eye contact can heighten conflict and hinder effective communication. Conversely, open and relaxed body language, active listening, and respectful gestures can promote understanding and facilitate peaceful resolutions. For instance, family members sitting together, facing each other, and maintaining open body language while calmly discussing a disagreement can create an atmosphere of trust and cooperation.

5. Non-Verbal Communication Patterns:

Families often develop their unique non-verbal communication patterns and rituals that are specific to their dynamics. These patterns can include inside jokes, shared gestures, or routines that convey meaning and strengthen the familial bond. For example, a particular facial expression or a specific hand gesture may be understood only within the family context, promoting a sense of belonging and fostering a shared identity.

6. Emotional Support and Empathy:

Non-verbal cues play a crucial role in providing emotional support and empathy within families. Facial expressions, body posture, and gentle touches can communicate understanding, compassion, and a willingness to listen. Active engagement through non-verbal cues fosters a sense of emotional safety and encourages family members to express their feelings and concerns. For instance, a family member leaning in, maintaining eye contact, and offering a comforting touch to another family member in distress conveys empathy and reassurance.

Conclusion:

Body language is a powerful tool in family dynamics, influencing communication, emotional connection, and overall well-being. By being attuned to non-verbal cues within the family unit, we can deepen understanding, foster stronger bonds, and create an environment of love, support, and open communication. Recognizing and responding to the non-verbal language of our family members allows us to build stronger connections, navigate conflicts effectively, and create a nurturing and harmonious family dynamic that promotes love, understanding, and growth.

Conclusion:

In this book, we have explored the fascinating world of body language and its profound impact on our lives. Body language serves as a universal language, speaking volumes about our thoughts, emotions, and intentions, even when we are silent. By understanding and interpreting the subtle cues and gestures, we can enhance our communication skills, build stronger relationships, and navigate social interactions with greater insight.

Throughout the chapters, we have delved into various aspects of body language, from decoding facial expressions and understanding gestures and postures to interpreting eye contact and recognizing non-verbal cues in different contexts. We have explored the nuances of body language in relationships, friendships, family dynamics, and even professional settings. Examples and explanations have provided practical insights, helping us apply this knowledge to our everyday lives.

By mastering body language, we gain a valuable tool for effective communication. We can build rapport, convey confidence, and foster understanding with others. We have learned to recognize both congruent and incongruent signals, enabling us to navigate social situations more accurately. Moreover, we have discussed the ethical considerations of reading and utilizing body language responsibly, promoting respect and empathy in our interactions.

Remember, body language is a dynamic and context-dependent form of communication. It varies across cultures, individuals, and situations. While we can gain valuable insights by observing and interpreting non-verbal cues, it is essential to consider multiple factors and exercise caution in making assumptions.

As we conclude this journey into the realm of body language, let us embrace the power of non-verbal communication as a means to connect, understand, and inspire others. By becoming more aware of our own body language and attuned to the signals of those around us, we can create meaningful connections, resolve conflicts with empathy, and express ourselves authentically.

May the knowledge gained from this book empower you to navigate social interactions with confidence, foster harmonious relationships, and deepen your understanding of the intricate ways in which we communicate without words. Let us embrace the rich tapestry of body language and continue to learn and grow in our ability to connect with others on a deeper level.

Remember, your body speaks louder than words, and with this newfound understanding, you hold the key to unlocking a world of enhanced communication and meaningful connections.

Additional Resources and Literature:

1. "THE DEFINITIVE Book of Body Language" by Allan Pease and Barbara Pease - This comprehensive guide explores various aspects of body language, including facial expressions, gestures, and postures, offering practical tips for interpreting and utilizing non-verbal cues.

2. "What Every BODY is Saying: An Ex-FBI Agent's Guide to Speed-Reading People" by Joe Navarro - Written by a former FBI agent, this book provides insights into reading body language and decoding non-verbal signals, drawing from the author's years of experience in conducting behavioral analysis.

3. "The Power of Body Language: How to Succeed in Every Business and Social Encounter" by Tonya Reiman - Tonya Reiman offers a comprehensive guide to understanding and utilizing body language to enhance communication, build rapport, and succeed in various personal and professional settings.

4. "Body Language: Learn How to Read Others and Communicate with Confidence" by Elizabeth Kuhnke - This book provides practical advice and techniques for reading body language accurately, improving communication skills, and building positive relationships in both personal and professional spheres.

5. "Influence: The Psychology of Persuasion" by Robert Cialdini - While not solely focused on body language, this book explores the principles of persuasion and influence, shedding light on how non-verbal cues can be used to persuade and influence others effectively.

6. Online Courses: Platforms like Udemy and Coursera offer online courses on body language and non-verbal communication. These courses provide in-depth knowledge, practical exercises, and additional resources to further enhance your understanding and application of body language skills.

7. Academic Journals and Research Papers: Explore academic journals and research papers in the fields of psychology, communication, and sociology to access the latest findings and studies on body language and non-verbal communication.

Remember, continuing to learn and explore the subject of body language is a lifelong journey. These resources and literature will serve as valuable references to deepen your understanding and further develop your skills in decoding and utilizing non-verbal cues. Happy exploring!

About the Author

My name is Rami and I am passionate about promoting the benefits of a vegan lifestyle through delicious and easy-to-make recipes, as well as tips and advice on how to incorporate a vegan lifestyle into your daily routine.

I became vegan for ethical, environmental, and health reasons, and I believe that a plant-based diet can improve the lives of both people and animals. On my books, you'll find a variety of vegan recipes that are not only delicious, but also easy to make. From breakfast to dinner and everything in between, my recipes are perfect for anyone looking to try veganism or to add more plant-based meals to their diet.

In addition to recipes, I will also be sharing tips and advice on how to make the transition to a vegan lifestyle as smooth as possible. Whether it's advice on finding vegan options when eating out, or suggestions for cruelty-free beauty and household products, I want to make it as easy as possible for you to live a compassionate and sustainable lifestyle.

I believe that a vegan diet and lifestyle can be delicious, varied, and easy to follow. I am constantly experimenting with new ingredients and techniques to create unique and delicious dishes that will inspire you to try veganism.

I hope you will join me on this journey of discovery and experimentation and will find my books helpful in your quest to live a more compassionate, healthy, and sustainable life.

Don't miss out!

Visit the website below and you can sign up to receive emails whenever Rami Georgiev publishes a new book. There's no charge and no obligation.

https://books2read.com/r/B-A-JXNW-BFWKC

BOOKS2READ

Connecting independent readers to independent writers.

Also by Rami Georgiev

The Ultimate Vegan European Recipe Book - From the Streets of Paris
to the Beaches of Greece
The Vegan Mindset: Living a Compassionate and Conscious Life
Vegan Beauty Made Easy
Vegan Parenting: Raising the Next Generation of Earth Stewards
Roaming for a Better World:
The Plant-Powered Athlete
Discovering Vegan India
The Path to Enlightenment
Karma in Action
Discovering Vegan France
Conversation with the Devil
Discovering Vegan China
Vegan Paradise in Bali
Discovering Vegan Italy:
Psychology Facts: How to Read People's Minds.
Unmasking the Shadows: Exploring the Depths of Dark Psychology
Confidence Unleashed
The Power of Words
The Silent Conversation: Mastering the Art of Body Language
The Conscious Connection: Unlocking the Secrets to Mindful
Relationships
Mindful Mastery
The Subconscious Mastery Blueprint

Embracing the Unvarnished Truth: 40 Truths About Human Relationships

Forty Paths to Happiness: Embrace Transformation, Leave the Past Behind, and Discover Joyful Living

The Art of Mind Reading: 40 Techniques for Unveiling Thoughts and Motivations

Stress Management: 35 Transformative Techniques to Prevent and Reduce Everyday Stress in Your Life

Transforming Habits: 40 Proven Strategies to Cultivate Positive Change in Your Life

Watch for more at vegandelights.space.

www.ingramcontent.com/pod-product-compliance
Lightning Source LLC
Chambersburg PA
CBHW031404160726
47993CB00003B/1104